One flew east

Carla Martin-Wood

What they're saying about *One flew east*

Joanne Uppendahl, Child and Family Counselor for 25 years, widely published poet, author of *She Who Gathers Stones*

"Be prepared to have your heart broken and reassembled. You will not be the same after reading these poems.

Tender, sad, but without a trace of self-pity, these poems will leave you speechless with admiration for the writer's candor and courage. I defy any reader to come away from this book without a deeper, more profound understanding of how we survive the pain of growing up in a dysfunctional family.

Carla Martin-Wood battles her giants and wins. She carries the reader on a journey, finally emerging *"unable to steer any other course but / away."* This book is bittersweet and profoundly moving. It is one of the finest collections of poetry I have read.

As a child and family counselor for 25 years, as well as a survivor of personal family trauma, I applaud this book, and am honored to recommend it to you. You won't forget what you read in these pages."

Zoë Guilherme, Former counselor of at-risk youth, Editor, *Triggerfish Critical Review*

"This book is an uncovering, a survivor's pursuit of understanding ...of gracious sharing ... of resolve ... of eventual peace. This is a *correct* write ... a necessary write ... riveting, vibrant, and brutal. With breathless astonishment, I can only say to you, this is a fist of a write!"

Margot Brown, Editor *Postcards from Eve* (Fortunate Childe Publications), author *Leave of Absence* (The Pink Petticoat Press)

"In her life-long journey to distill and transform pain into inner clarity, then poetic expression, Carla Martin-Wood's work retains its artistic integrity. *One flew east* documents the mind-numbing experiences of the survivor of an abusive childhood, one who has healed herself by summoning memories – slivers of Light, Magick, and the redemptive qualities of some of her own abusers – and exorcising the rest. This accessible collection has the potential to ignite similar healing for those who aspire to do the same."

Wendy A. Howe, Pushcart Prize nominee, widely published poet, former Editor, *The Baroque Review*

"*One flew east* is a powerful collection of poems relating the raw, emotional experiences that shaped a family's history. It is a portrait study of life and the environment that defines its children. Riveting and realistic, this is a work that will leave you haunted and thinking long after the initial reading."

Lise Whidden, Pushcart Prize nominee and widely published poet

"Carla Martin-Wood continues to inspire and captivate us with honest images of real people in their most intimate environments. This incredible book of poems is a must read for anyone who has survived childhood."

Sandy Benitez, Editor of *The Red Poppy Review* and *Flutter Poetry Journal,* Publisher and Editor, Flutter Press

"Carla Martin-Wood is a survivor, and it's clearly apparent in this compelling book of poetry. *One flew east* takes the reader along on her personal journey through family heartache, relationships, abuse, disappointments, and death, resulting in a woman strengthened by it all."

Karen Kelsay, Editor, *Victorian Violet Press & Journal*, Editor and Publisher, White Violet Press and Aldrich Publishing

"*I survived/ I survived/ I survived.* This is the mantra of sadness and joy Carla Martin-Wood sings to the world through her book *One flew east*. In sections titled *Heroes* and *Monsters,* the contrast between figures is staggering. It underscores how even the smallest positive interaction can become an indelible impression of hope."

Carol Lynn Grellas, four-time Pushcart Prize nominee, author of *Litany of Finger Prayers* (Pudding House Press 2009), *Object of Desire* (Finishing Line Press 2008), and *A Thousand Tiny Sorrows* (March Street Press)

"Carla Martin-Wood's collection of poems guides us with elegiac grace through a journey that is not only frightening, but also astoundingly brave. *One flew east* is a shrewd, yet honest examination of one woman's fight to endure against all odds, where even in the midst of mourning that which cannot be changed, forgiveness seems to come. This astonishing collection teeters ever so warily between love and loss; as the poem *For Montine* so poignantly states – *to you: whom I hated, whom I loved.*"

Cover and interior photograph: *Four Crows,* ©2012, Brenda Levy Tate

Graphic Illustration, *Crows Perched On A Silhouetted Tree*, ©2012, KJ Pargeter, licensed through ClipartOf.com/KJ Pargeter/28236

Fortunate Childe Publications

2012

My thanks to Margot Brown for her editorial insight,
to Brenda Levy Tate for her incomparable photography
and astute commentary,
and to both for their invaluable friendship.

This book is for all the lambs.

Little Lamb, who made thee?
Dost thou know who made thee?
– William Blake

L'Innocence, William-Adolphe Bouguereau

The Poems

I: Oracle

II: Shadows

III: Heroes

IV: Myths & Legends

The Poems

V: Monsters

VI: Aftermath

VII: Postcards

Preface

A dozen near-identical dresses hanging on a rack can assume very different shapes and appearances when worn by twelve individual women. No two will find themselves reflected in similar posture, or wear their matching designs with equal grace. Some will accept what they see and take it home with them; the rest will put it back.

Thus it is with survivors, not only those who have emerged from abusive histories but also those whose challenges have arisen from elsewhere. They wrap themselves in their own stories: almost any traumatic situation will possess elements in common with others, yet in the end, it is the protagonist in his or her own narrative who fleshes out its contours and determines its final impact on character.

Sadly, some confront their mirror-selves and see only victims' faces staring back - forever diminished by past pain, forever struggling to cast off the limitations of bitterness too long held close, of scars too often examined and opened fresh. Theirs are tight bindings, never altered to embrace them more gently.

Carla Martin-Wood has transformed her own off-the-rack garment from stained and torn cloth into an astonishing creation. Now shared through the medium of poetry, its effect on the reader is unforgettable. One might almost say "lovely", but the events recounted in many of these poems are far from beautiful. Yet she has risen above them and mended every tear, with each stitch and line and wrinkle binding the whole. She stands before us clothed in strength.

This is a gown she cannot now set aside, even if she wished to do so. She carries its folds with pride and authority, the various flashing and clashing colors swirling around her. She even invites us to try it on for a brief look at our own reflections. For some of us, the style and material will make for an uncomfortably close fit. Others will frown and murmur, "No, that just isn't *me*" – in itself a valuable admission.

And that abandoned rack – *imagine how many levels of meaning lurk in that one word!* – lies empty, its burden remembered but long since discarded.

Brenda Levy Tate

Pushcart Prize nominee, author of *Wingflash* (The Pink Petticoat Press, 2011), *Cleansing* (Rising Tide Press, 2005) and *Beeline* (Lopside Press, 2007), and included in *Jailbreaks: 99 Canadian Sonnets* (Biblioasis 2008), an anthology of the editors' favorite Canadian sonnets of the past century.

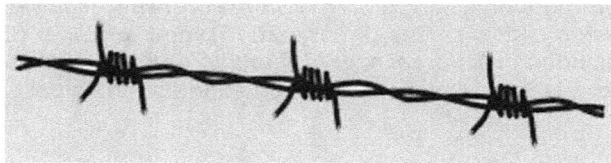

I
Oracle

Mary Frances

When I was small
each morning they dressed me
in petticoats and patent shoes
to visit Mary Frances
my Great Granny
who sat all day
in her dark room
back to the door
brushing and braiding
her long black hair
over and over
keeping it pristine
against any worldly thing
that might have touched
or tangled

windows shuttered
shades drawn
rivulets of infectious tears
flowed neverending
down her face expressionless
ageless and untouched by life
though she was eighty

she only spoke
to me once
it was a child's voice

she said I was an angel
too good to live
in this world

she left for heaven soon after
and I imagined Jesus
drying all those tears

Mama-Teen took photos
of Mary Frances in her coffin
people sang
and the preacher said
the angels did, too
for she was righteous

when we got home
they gave me her room
and when the moon rose bright
shadows of the sycamore
branched across my wall
casting a strange and troubled alphabet
I already feared to read.

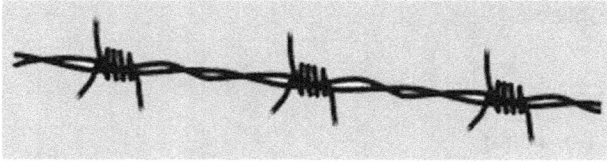

II

Shadows

Vespers at Mama-Teen's*

Safe beneath quilted coverlets,
sweet with lavender and sun,
I sink to slumber
in a world of summer lullabies,
see the moon,
naked and caught like a pearl
in the net of a sycamore tree,
while somewhere
an owl hoots low, frogs croak, crickets hum,
and her voice, cracked with age,
sings from the old piano,
peace, be still for me,
as a gathering storm
moves in from the sea,
and I sleep sound
though not a stone is silent.

Until I entered first grade, I called my grandmother "Mama-Teen" – an affectionate appellation, derived from her given name, Montine. – CMW

Sacred Harp

for Lise Whidden

Mama-Teen directed the singing
at the Free Will Baptist Church
and she didn't hold with fancified music
like *Rise Up, O Men of God*
anthem of the high-falutin'
Methodists down the road
She was grooming me for an alto
in the Sacred Harp chorus
no instruments tolerated nohow
just the book
with its odd-shaped notes
and the vocal chords
God gave you

She broke in a run
dragging me behind
and grabbed ol' Brother Johnson
by the hand
shaking it hard

Lordy, Preacher!
Somewhere in that message this mornin'
you quit preachin'
and went slap on
to messin' in my personal business.
Praise Jesus!
I sure do thank you.

He'd preached on divorce
and I knew
she was thinking about my mama
who provoked whistles and catcalls
when she pranced down the street
in her new halter dress
flashing a smile
like Rita Hayworth
on the movie poster
downtown

Mom was newly freed
from husband two
soon to find number three
and poor Mama-Teen would crane
her ostrich neck
to see out the windows
anytime a date brought her home

Now Brother Johnson himself
had confirmed her suspicion
that divorce was an abomination
Mama-Teen believed
he was the very domicile
of the Holy Ghost
that morning
preaching a directed truth
signed and sealed
no chance it could be other

She spotted an old friend
and pulled me on behind her

My sweet Jesus – it's Sister Jordan!
How long has it been girl?
Have mercy, Maybelle,
The folks you see
when you don't have a handgun!

Later on the grounds
that indolent summer afternoon
our stomachs filled after an orgy
of BBQ and Sister Gordo's potato salad
after talking for hours
about which neighbors
were going to hell for what sin
and who was pregnant
or divorced
or even just thinking about it
we'd have a singing

Mama-Teen would wave
to hush the crowd
a cross made of people would form
and voices
in strangely beautiful harmonies
would rise
lifting the righteous
in premature rapture
straight on up
to heaven's gate.

When I was Isaac

for all the lambs

August tent revival
last Sunday night service
hypertensive preacher
ruddy countenance and hair
sweaty face swelled to bursting
told the tale of Isaac
with gleeful passion

How instead of a lamb
Abraham placed him on that altar

Praise you, Lord!

How Isaac waited
for the knife to fall

Yes, Lord – Hallelujah!

How God stopped the hand of Abraham

Praise Jesus!

How later Jesus came
and was the blood sacrifice

Amen and Amen!

Back home
I sang with all the zeal
of a five year old
dosed up on religion
Are you washed
in the blood
in the soul cleansing blood
of the Lamb?

In the kitchen
Mama-Teen sliced ham
on the butcher block
while my mom told her
Bob Korman was on his way
to pick her up

No, Dorice – not that Jew boy!

And just as I reached up
for a slice of ham
Mama-Teen grabbed me from behind
I thought for a hug
but couldn't hug back
facing out like that
as she pressed the butcher knife
against my throat
If you go, I'll do it
I swear I will
I don't swear lies, Dorice!

I remember
how everything moved real slow
how still I became
Isaac's story in my head
wondering if it was the same
for that boy
this numbing peace
eyes open wide and docile
no fear
not even when my mom
slammed the screen door
behind her

Mama-Teen stood there
blade against my throat
when Papa slipped up behind
his hand stopping mayhem
and gently removed
her fingers from the hilt

Knife relinquished
she walked the long hall
to her bedroom alone
without a word

Papa put his arms around me
sat with me a long time
It's ok now, Baby Gal

I remember
how I thought

Mama-Teen was sick some way
wondered if Abraham was sick
with the same thing
if Isaac knew like I did
wondered if Jesus was a Jew
why Bob Korman was bad
and why faith needs blood

Finally, I fell asleep wondering
where lambs go
when they die.

Seeking spring

I have no love for death
kicked that unwanted suitor in the balls
stormed from my grandmother's side
unforgivably undead and
drinking from life's jugular
in great hungry gulps

my grandmother lived in winter
even in youth frost hung on her breath

I lived with her
a recalcitrant rose thin and frail
refusing to bloom like my sisters
they danced away with Mother
and I was left behind that year
in chilled silence
that bitter house
windchimes never stirred
in that dark place
though in the deepnight
trying windows
trying doors
wind wept like an orphan

now she lies in silence
thin blue veil draped icily
about her shoulders
and I must bundle up to pay a visit

later I plant marigolds

furiously

snapdragons

desperately

sunny tulips

death-defying daffodils

windchimes singing singing

snatch up houseplants and repot

never again to be potbound

plant sweetheart roses

it is too early

pots of herbs

mint for health

basil for love

this is mania

rosemary for protection

this is frenzy

crave the smell of greening earth

dig fingers deep in black soil

seek spring

conjure it

from myself

grope the earth with trembling hands

like a woman who wakes

from a nightmare of mastectomy

and searches to find

her own reassuring breast.

For Montine

I want to go back
to ham and potato salad Sundays
to piano lessons and the wincing pain
of your boar bristle brush
as it ripped through tangled curls

to lavender cologne and Juicy Fruit breath
that choked me as you imprisoned tender skin
in crinoline and fastened too tight
Mary Janes

to furtive bed checks
guarding against forbidden comic books
and phone calls from boys

to pins sticking into my waist
as you tried your latest designs on me

to hiding in the neighbor's cellar with every storm
because it was your only excuse to visit

to holding clothespins while you hung
broad white sails infused with summer sun

to gnarled hands filling my uplifted apron
with pungent sun-and-earth tomatoes
and strawberries that dripped guilty
down my chin

to vinegar-scented Easter eggs
and baby chicks an unnatural pink and purple
already doomed

to Howdy Doody till 9 a.m.
when we caught the bus
and went to town every Saturday
for no good reason

to your gaunt face
peering between curtains when I got home late

and even to the bible thumping
that drove me crazy
John 3:16, John 3:16
till you breathed your last
though I wasn't there to hear it

I want a voice
that can scream *I'm sorry*
loud enough so you can hear me
in heaven
or hell
or rotting in the dirt
wherever you are now

I want a map back to that place
because it went away so fast
before I could understand it
before I knew it was important
before I knew I would miss it like a lost limb

I want a way to turn on my heels
that are headed nowhere anyway
and run back to all those things – to you:
whom I hated, whom I loved.

Late prayer to Isis for my grandmother's soul

Comes she now, Isis

my grandmother
seven years old alone
tending a house of brothers

this tiny one
who stood on a chair
to cook and clean
ruled by a stern father
his heart fashioned
from coal he mined

comes she now

this little one
given charge of a houseful of boys
blamed for their misdeeds
chastised for their shortcomings

and when the youngest wandered
to forbidden tracks
beyond bleak fields
gone down for winter
it was not bloody Set
but man's machine
that brought him down

comes now this innocent
barefoot and weeping
shrouded in guilt undeserved

sent to retrieve
what the coal train left
in its wake
remnants of a brother for burial
bloody clothing
bits of flesh
almost nothing
gathered in her mending basket
as though needle and thread
might repair

and older she grew
and hardened of heart
like the coal
within her father's chest

grandchildren followed
our milk seasoned with bitter herbs
our lullabies sung in a minor key

comes she now in age to you

O Isis, great Mother God,
wrap this one gentle in your wings
remember how you resurrected
your brother great Osiris
how you journeyed

to gather the fourteen pieces
grave Set had made of him
how you recreated him
as the moon waxed full
remember how you sang him back
from darkness

take pity then upon this child
who had no magicks
and knew no song
who walked alone
with her mending basket

sing to her, O Isis
O Mother God
sing her into wholeness.

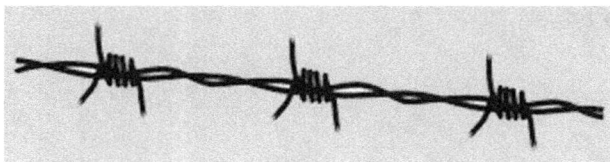

III

Heroes

Fishing

When I was nine
in pre-dawn darkness,
silent but for occasional ruffle
of waking bird's feathers or small splash
as dragonfly became breakfast
for some iridescent wonder,
Papa and I crouched quiet
at lake's edge, waiting
for catfish to nibble.

I knew Papa was thinking
how he'd skin it, fry it up,
while already I was thinking
how that dragonfly was prey for fish
that would soon be on our table,
how that meant something really important
that I'd figure out later.
But it slipped away
because it was Saturday,
and I was happy
with Papa all to myself,
no siblings to scramble for attention
and Mama with other fish to fry.

As light took the sky,
trees became scaffolds I climbed
to watch anonymous forms beneath the water,

till snared and gasping on a hook,
everything had a name.

He talked till evening
about things I didn't understand,
Gene Tunney, Gillette razors, the lady
who worked at Woolworth's lunch counter,
and I talked about things he didn't understand,
Howdy Doody, my Tiny Tears doll, the boy
with freckles in my English class,
love translating every mysterious word.

Later, drawing near home under a high hunter's moon,
I saw something I'd never noticed in his eyes,
something that struggled for life
like the fish he lifted from the lake,
something lonely.

Funeral

You did not attend.

You were not found
in words hewn from rough stone
brought down from the burning mount polished

nor in the undanceable song

nor in the odd brightness
of those sad flowers

most of all, you were not
in that strange form
lying in the elegant jewel case

You were walking with me
when I was six
and we found treasure
deep in the singing wood
a glistering case of chitin
legs still clinging
to the bark of a redbud
translucent shell
of the cicada
all glory gone
to fly against the wind.

Papa's Finale

Always a dancer at heart,
from the swing in your step
to the occasional jig
to amuse or embarrass us.

Then cancer called the tune
and left you still.

That night, we huddled around the old table,
every dysfunctional child,
another mute, self-involved meal,
but served with a darker silence,
an individual grief.

Then stillness shattered.

Your old blackthorn walking stick
leaned against the hearth,
useless these three years.
We startled when we heard it
rap against the wall, a sharp tapping,
and something
vibrations of the house, passing traffic
caused it to stand upright,
dance in quick staccato,
then fall back again.

Skittish laughter all round,

disbelief, smart remarks,
but I knew.

You were dancing
down the Milky Way,
strutting like a sailor on leave,
doing your mad Irish jig
from the Moon
to the rings of Saturn,
a Texas reel at the edge of Time,
a wild Tennessee clog,
a crazy Cajun two-step
straight into the arms of God.

Sally of Willendorf*

In memoriam, Sally Brown

You hid all the children of the world
behind your amazingly graceful skirts
beside your ebony enormity
I safely grew and safely slept
and rode that Nile that flowed eternal
from your heart of bright darkness
and basked in the Eden-light
that shone like a secret sun
from those chocolate eyes

When you danced
mountains shook
when you sang
storms fled in terror

I remember how you
came rising from my childhood once
to slap me down
on a Birmingham pavement
convincing others on those
Nationally Guarded streets
that we were fighting
made them think I was some
white chick good 'ol girl
and saved me from jail that time

We fought
and you yelled
about how you knew *your place*
that these young upstarts were wrong
I screamed back that you taught me
this responsibility without words
fed me with that bounty
that grew in the wilds of your spirit
made me strong in my beliefs

We fought after that for years
until one day you called me
saying what I will never forget
that you were proud of me
I said you should know your place
Sally of Willendorf
your place is Mt. Olympus

Sally of Willendorf
feeder of young souls
protector of the helpless
teacher of power
you grow in my children
you sing in my poems
you dance in my faith
you live in the begonias
that will bless my Spring!

The Venus of Willendorf is one of the earliest known representations of the Mother Goddess.

For Herbert

in memoriam

When I was seven
you read my poems
filled with knights and castles
everything but the truth

when I was nine
and believed I didn't exist
you said I was a writer
gave me an identity
something to hold onto
when earth quaked

because of you
I understood
why Mr. Smith's willow
did not fall
like the big maple
when tornadoes
whipped through one spring

because of you
I could relax
a day or two
when you'd visit Mother
bring me new books
brush my hair tenderly
like a father

you took us to the zoo
bought me cotton candy
and when a yellowjacket
stung me
while looking for his share
you took tobacco
from Mother's cigarette
made a poultice
stopped the sting
like some magick trick

later, when Mother died
someone said
you sat beside her coffin
but everything was so dark
I couldn't see

time passed
I grew up
you grew old
and I searched
till I found you
wrote to thank you
for being an island
a lighthouse
a savior
my last knight

for years we stayed in touch
by phone
and glorious cards you sent

then the phone went silent
the mailbox went empty
and you were gone
following after Mother
like always

I don't need your DNA
to be your child
the years you watched over me
and followed as Mother moved
from place to place
from one brutal bastard to the next
the engagement ring
you gave me to keep
when Mother refused your proposal
those are the legacies
that make me
your daughter.

For David with apologies

You were a drunk, too
but unlike the others
you called my Mom *Angel*
and that's how you treated her

you couldn't hold a job
and she was an executive
traveling the country
while you stayed home
with Grandmother and Papa
called them *Mom* and *Dad*
because you never had either

never a Saturday passed
when you didn't work
on some old car
with me on the front seat
pretending to help

I hung around
trying to figure you out
waiting for it all
to fall apart

Start the car, you'd say
race the engine
turn it off
start it again, sweetie

I thought I was cool
we'd play the radio loud
and laugh
then you'd give me two quarters
for an allowance

in winter
you drove me from school
through waist-high snowbanks
because I had asthma
or cramps
(though it embarrassed me
that you knew)

on my birthday
you gave me bongo drums
and a guitar
then taught me to bop
and jitterbug
to Little Richard

Grandmother said
it was the devil's music
but she laughed at us
trying to dance
while Papa grabbed
his old blackthorn shillelagh
and did a jig
said Little Richard
was Black Irish

you loved us all
anyone could see it
and I didn't know
what to make of you

in spring
Mom met Julio
citizen of the world
who played the piano
and her

in summer
she sent me
to tell you to go
sent a child
to break your heart

when I grew up
and you'd grown old
I looked for you

but you were gone
deep into a bottle
shattered
by a fifteen year old
following directions.

To the neighbor in North Carolina

I haven't forgotten you
though we spoke only once

You taught at my school
and when you spotted me in the office
withdrawing from classes
eyes swelled from crying all night
heard me explain that we were moving again
you asked me to come for a visit

there was a big portrait
of your late husband
and another of your daughter
in her wedding gown
you showed me her room
with its stereo and records
its white bed and frilly pillows
desk and bookcase just so

you said things were empty now
you had plenty of room
for another little girl
you said I'd be doing you a favor
to take that room and make it mine
so you wouldn't feel so all alone
that I could live with you
and finish school
in those mountains that I loved

I said *no thanks* that day
accepted the snack you offered
chatted about nothing, and left

part of me wanted to say yes
part of me wanted to be taken care of
instead of worrying all the time
not yet sixteen, part of me needed to rest
but I was afraid
for my brother, my sisters, my mother
if I weren't around

I wasn't in your class
I'd never met you
couldn't imagine why
you'd want someone like me
a stranger tracking mud
on your white carpet

older now, I realize you must have known
must have seen my mother's bruises
heard the small explosions
that rocked our lives
in that house

now I want to thank you
for noticing
for trying
to be a hero.

IV

Myths & Legends

Photo of my mother at nineteen

Slender, sepia, almost-child
you lean against a tree, unidentifiable
beside hollyhocks in Grandmother's front yard

slip of nothing, dress a wisp of gauze
eyes gazing far off, so intentionally wistful
perhaps your last attempt at make-believe

unaware – never knowing I was there
ugly clump of cells, undeniable
hiding inside the pristine self of you
dividing, multiplying

I must apologize for my poor math
my presence heavy, uninvited
taking without asking, bits of you
in magically woven double-helix intricacy

I love this ancient photograph
creased, cracked
your name written in blue child-script
too open – loops and curlicues
an autograph perhaps for some new love
I love this photograph of you
taken while war raged across the world
and you danced to Glenn Miller in USO-blivion

I love this photograph of you
your face, before you knew.

Werewolf

When I was seven and you in your twenties,
late one night, you perched in the arms
of that old sycamore outside my window,
wearing a cloud of gown
that shifted opalescent in the shadows.
Bright hair drifted about your face;
you lifted your voice to the pearl moon,
howled,
clear and cold as any wolf.

Next morning you hummed,
made pancakes, used the good china,
opened morning-glory curtains to yellow sunshine.
And when I asked if you were a werewolf,
you said I'd dreamed it. I said like hell I did,
and tasted Ivory soap and maple syrup
all the way to school.

You changed after that, became fierce.
Swapped making pancakes for pancake makeup,
prowled canyons flanked by skyscrapers,
went for the jugular,
nailed down deals with 4-inch stilettos,
signed contracts in lipstick.

For years, I wondered at your transformation,
and why you did that –
sat in a tree, stared at the moon,

howling
like nobody's mother.

When it was too late to tell you, I remembered
how fear came into our lives,
how I found your oils and brushes in the trash,
how mangled paintings went up in flames
that reached for the moon,
how the piano grew silent, and you forgot to dance,
and no one laughed too loudly or sang.

How on the night he finally left,
you climbed the sycamore easy as a child,
sat there howling at the stars.

Skydiver

In your 51-year freefall
you feared nothing but gravity
whatever held you down, fenced you in, made you stop

never once considered that impactful moment
when birdboned body meets stone
always knew an updraft would save you
relied on the reprieve of air currents
you could ride awhile

floated arms out, waiting for evening magic
when warm air from the valley
buoyed you upward into the sunset

lifted effortless through Maxfield Parrish clouds
nothing tugged at you
called you back from the edge of the atmosphere

then at night, silvered and soaring, light as a dream
I never doubted you
fed pearls to the moon till it grew full
then lit the stars
like votives in the sky

came the day downdrafts betrayed you
how surprised you must have been
when earth opened her arms to embrace you.

Sunday Mom Blues

Turquoise pink kitchen circa '55
morning light filtered
through fresh washed linen
flapping on the line outside
dappled pastel walls with sun

smell of wax spun
on that old turntable
background scratch pop hiss
as Bird made his axe
sing sweet and blue
played *Summertime*
with notes to make even baby Jesus
want to slow dance on Sunday

then the Andrews'
Boogie Woogie Bugle
you laughed *C'mon Sister*
twirled me around
(never *daughter*/ never *child*
Sister didn't make people
look for crow's feet
or guess your age)

we made thumbprint cookies
you filling the hollows with bittersweet
chocolate and raspberry jam
as I stood watchful
for errant dribbles

later in the living room
we hung poppies you'd painted
on panels of washed silk
didn't speak
listened to opera on the radio
didn't understand a word
wept anyway

me dreading tomorrow
and stilettos that clicked you away
to the waiting plane.

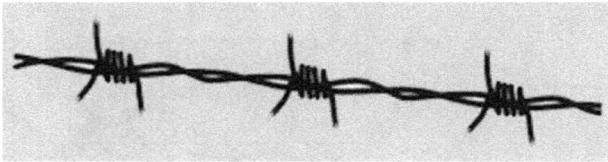

V

Monsters

Jimmy

I was three
when Mother said
you were my new daddy

I saw you sitting
in Grandmother's porch rocker
and fascinated by your hair
Cherokee black and shiny
I patted it gently
kissed your arm
and said:
My new daddy has pretty hair

you slapped me off the porch
yelled *I'm not your daddy*

I landed in a rosebush
and Grandmother ran to get
the burning stuff
she put on cuts

Mother took me
to live in your house
where Grandmother fed me at night
through my bedroom window
This is our secret
be my little birdy, now
tweet, tweet
open wide

later I found out
you didn't want to feed
a child who wasn't yours
you measured all the food
every morning
wrote it down
measured again when you returned

afternoons were happy
Mother painted
and let me watch
she made a boy on a bridge
a wedding
and me
appear from her brush
like magick

I sat in my swing
she talked to me
about bobwhites
and redbirds
told me to be still
while she sketched me

when you found the painting
of me with my unacceptable
strawberry hair
you burned everything
her paints
and brushes

all the pictures
I thought
you'd burn me, too
so I went to live
with my grandparents

when I was five
Mother left you
brought my new sister
moved into my grandparents' house
you came to get her
and Papa wouldn't let you in

I hid behind the hedges
with my toy bow and arrows

when you scratched off
tires leaving long black streaks
on the pavement
I shot at you
over and over
till you disappeared.

What Kenneth did

I do not know what Kenneth did
I only know what Sally said
If Kenneth did what Sally said
Don't want to know what Kenneth did

Some things happen
that settle into our bones
deep in the marrow
where thoughts never go

Mom married the big marine
and brought him home
when I was seven

he took me on his lap
and I watched the sunset
over his shoulder

after that
I always thought
the sun went down
because it couldn't bear
to watch the world
anymore

then Sally came in
threw him to the floor
tried to kill him

I never knew why
only that I was afraid
and for years after
I cried every time I saw
the sun go down

I knew she saw something
I didn't see
I heard them say
she could have been lynched
an uppity Negro woman
hitting a white man
hard like that
throwing him out of the house

next day he took my mother
sister and my new baby brother
they moved to Albany
while I stayed behind
with Grandmother's quilting bees
Papa's bunnies
Sally's laughter and lemonade

I never saw Kenneth again
and I was glad
last thing I heard
he'd run off to Canada

when I had children of my own
Sally appeared one day
we talked till almost dark

she rocked my baby
mentioned Kenneth once
and was surprised
that I remembered nothing

I do not know what Kenneth did
I only know what Sally said
If Kenneth did what Sally said
Don't want to know what Kenneth did.

I hate you Julio Varone

I waited till I was sure you were dead
till the calendar said no way
you could still breathe
then I threw a party
for myself
danced like Rumplestiltskin
stomping my feet and ranting

I hate you Julio Varone
blue-footed bastard
padding like an old woman
down the morning hall
farting loudly in your long girly robe
holding your coffee mug
like a cup of the Queen's tea
pinky up
you who put the knot in our guts
and the stopper in our mouths
slayer of our youth
cancer on our future

I hate you Julio Varone
for every time you hit our mother
for your honeymoon in Norfolk
when you bashed her face
on the corner of an air conditioner
and I didn't recognize her
when she came home that night

I hate you Julio Varone
because you made my mother
a caricature
a drunk
so that when you hauled us out
of bed on Christmas Eve
to scrub the walls with our toothbrushes
then told us there would be no presents
and gave us moldy wieners
for Christmas dinner
our mother slept through it all

I hate you Julio Varone
because I caught you putting pills
in her mouth as she lay drunk
she choked on them
and I had to clear her throat
with my fingers
and when I hoarded ten dollars
to buy her a Mother's Day gift
you hit me hard
and said she didn't deserve it

I hate you Julio Varone
because you wouldn't call the doctor
for my brother and he almost died
that awful night in North Carolina
and he's dead now for real
from the ugliness you put inside him
like a black light

that shone through his eyes
and distorted everything good

I hate you Julio Varone
because you killed Sam
my cat for eleven years
threw her from the window of our car
flying down the Jersey Turnpike
shattered fragile bones
ripped open fur
that had been my comfort
splashed her blood
on a highway altar
and I could not even weep

I hate you Julio Varone
because you turned from the window
to my baby sister
and shouted *You're next if you don't shut up*
and I hate you because you meant it
I hate you because
if you hadn't passed out
on the highway shoulder
you'd have done it

I hate you Julio Varone
for saying my sisters were lesbians
when we didn't know what that meant
I hate you for telling me that if I loved them
I must be one too

and for saying
You'll die a whore in a dirty motel room

I hate you Julio Varone
for making me write the checks
to pay our bills
when I was only fifteen
and should have been thinking
about lipstick or rock bands
or dope
or hell – anything but being
the devil's bookkeeper
terrified of errors

I hate you Julio Varone
for throwing our grandparents
out on the street
after they'd sold their home
and had nowhere to go
I hate you for causing my grandfather's stroke
when he tried to wrestle you to the ground
to save us
I hate you for sowing
the cruel seeds
of his death

You were Caligula and Ivan the Terrible
and Hitler and Genghis Kahn
and Stalin and Idi Amin
you were my nightmare
you were my hell

with quagmires of feces
and blue sulfur flames
you were Jack Torrance
and Freddy Kreuger

I hate you Julio Varone
for making our home your personal Dachau
with four frightened inmates
till I discovered
bad boys in black leather
who threatened to kill you
in the alley one night
and you ran
because that's what bullies do

We never saw you again
only the damage
like wreckage
from a hurricane
children who were not
futures tainted
fear and mistrust and failure
and the neverending anger
of the lambs

Here is your curse old man
here is your damnation
here is your hell
I survived
I survived
I survived.

VI

Aftermath

Midnight errand

Down a darkened alleyway
honeysuckle ladders up
rough hewn doorframes
and stucco walls
crumbling and grey
consecrated by misguided urine

Mickwee's Bar

smelling of stale beer and smoke
inhabited by the unenviable
who have fallen this far
to spin sketchy yarns
of the deified past
where lack of light and sobriety
camouflages liar and lie

somewhere in the darkness
my mother arches her back
and laughs
believes the lies
trusts

I will come
after homework
timid and fearful
to take her home.

Thurisaz*

I recall our house in Babylon
listening to the sea without/within
knowing myself alone
with fatherless child
weeping beneath the goose down quilt
a grief that could not share
itself or show itself entirely

My mother
who never cuddled
or diapered
or sang
who mothered me from boardrooms
and hotel rooms
from cocktail parties
and airport lounges
from pages of letters and
books she sent
who left that life for a man
who would betray her
and now lived her days
displaced and bewildered
wordless in that darkness
she crept into my bed
held me
rocking in the nightwomb
rocking in that rhythm
that speaks woman

crooning that ancient song of
mourning and life that binds
generation to generation

Upon that bed the three of us
till daybreak
one unborn
one who would bear
one who had borne
all fetal
curled in submission
knowing birth inevitable
fearing what rough hands
would drag us forth
and make us breathe.

*Thurisaz is the Rune meaning danger, pain to women, challenge, yet also
protection and gateway to new life.*

Cursed

I only wanted you to see
me. The unbeautiful
daughter, dutiful caretaker
of siblings, overseer
of household budgets
at fifteen, overlooked
midnight fetcher of the inebriated
dependable honor student
dull debater of politics
shy writer of poems
unwanted, misunderstood
never the perfect features
nor cozy tête á têtes
you shared with my sister
all gossip and magazine giggles
over cigarettes and scotch

Those last days in CICU
I barely left your side
wanted to take you home
put you back together
have you to myself awhile
hoping you would see

me, I unearthed artifacts
from myself, excavated mysteries
hieroglyphic fragments of my life
poems and photographs

a poster from a play of mine
that you'd attended drunk
recordings of short stories
made for the Blind School
when I was fourteen
newspaper clippings, reviews
recipes, my turquoise collection
even a secret affair
relics from the ruins of me
I dragged into the light
craving acknowledgement

Instead, you asked to see
a PBS celebration
of Egypt, our one common ground

Fiery August sunset
cast dappled gold
on hospital grey
and for a moment
we almost stood together

in sharp and holy shadows
of those great pyramids
as treasures unseen for millennia
emerged into sunlight
illuminated on tomb walls
writings indecipherable
and the painted pantheon

Winged Isis and Bast
Horus, Osiris, Ma'at
bejeweled belongings
of ancient ones
who walked the earth
as gods and kings

I waited to hear
an exclamation from you
a word I might stretch
into an evening's conversation

Yet you lay silent as Meretseger
still as though struck by her cobra
who curses with blindness those who see
sacred contents of the tombs
your hand groped wildly for mine
your voice so small and lost:

I cannot see.
I cannot see you.

Isa*

When my mother died
a polar chill began
that shuddered its way
from my solar plexus
to each compass point
so that I filled a tub
with scalding water
sinking in
to my chin
and did not find warmth
although it was the 10th of August.

Winter mourned a path
into my soul
howled at its center
keening and cold
scattered realities
leaving life
brittle and dry.

And I recalled
an amputee I'd met
who had a dark obsession
concerning the fate
of his missing leg
he swore he felt it moving
late at night and
could not sleep.

The dead are like this

I thought

and sank a little deeper

into the water

cold as winter earth.

Isa is the Rune meaning standstill, ice, the frozen time

Why I never visit

I don't visit that place
where pale fingers that glided over piano keys
imparting Mozart to the unattuned
go down to nothingness,
where flaming hair is finally quenched,
and porcelain skin sinks to alabaster bone,
where amber eyes are perpetually closed
seeing everything.

I don't bring flowers,
remembering your voice when I was four:
baby girl, don't pick those – they'll die.

I don't go there.
You never stayed in one place
more than a few weeks anyway.

I thought you visited me once
in a recovery room where I almost didn't,
pieces of you: cool fingers on my brow, slim white ankles,
as black stilettos clicked you out of the room
when I was coming to. A dream, they said.

I don't go there.
I like to think you got bored waiting
and found something better to do,
a place more interesting to go.

Letter to my mother, *in absentia*

In your incalculable absence
I find you everywhere
hiding in my pocket
like a lost key
to a door that opens
on an inscrutable garden
or a ribbon
meant to mark a place
in a book
I never really read

I follow
the breadcrumb trail
to nowhere
your hairbrush
golden locket
half-used lipstick
broken earring
hiss and crackle
of an old record
you used to play

that you are gone
is unacceptable

ghost winged luna
pale petals of celadon
pressed wistfully

against my window
or that bright cardinal
that lit upon my railing
bear messages I sense
but cannot understand

shadows grow long
yearn towards the mountain
fingers of purple twilight
stretch across the valley
hills rise like islands
in the mist

though evening comes
with drowsy choir
of cricket and frog
sleep only breeds confusion
you tease
at the edges of my dreams
and I almost see you
dressed all in white
we have tea
in a bright outdoor café
Caruso singing
somewhere in the background
till morning scatters night
and I remember
nothing.

From the shadows

Draw shadows first
not lines, not light
everything that makes
a face its own
is in the shadows

an artist
Mother tried in vain to teach me
how to make life leap
from faces sketched
with charcoal on rough paper

down the years
I hear her words
and know them true

for never the light
of sun dappled spring
nor summer's bright bazaar
nor autumn's grace
nor winter-dazzled white
could sketch this face
I've come to wear
oh no –
it was the storm
it was the night.

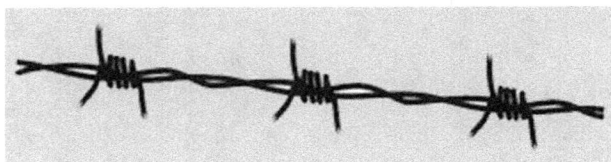

VII

Postcards

Casting lots

Always a gambler
she usually lost
but that never stopped her
Mother cast us kids out
into this world like dice
three came up snake eyes
fast and hard
leaving me
poised on edge
forever waiting
for a strong wind to come
whipping through the open doors
of this casino
or the hard black rhythm
of a good blues band
to shake the walls of this joint
and make me tumble
I swear sometimes at night
I hear my mother's voice
come singing off-key
and slurred a little through
the smoky dreams in this place
and it pisses me off
that she's not here to watch
'cuz I can feel a seven coming up
I just know it in my bones.

Crow Sisters

We shared a Dachau
and no one
really walks away from that

its shadows grab at your ankles
trip you up
no matter how hard you try
to dance like everyone else
it technicolors every nightmare

we survive
but never live through it
our gladdest moments
tainted just enough
to make them less than
real

the toxic tattoo
that marked our holo-
caustic youth
sank deep into our veins
mutated us
into crows
ravens
never the skylarks
we might have been

my sister scavenges castoffs
at thrift shops
on the side of the road
in alleyways
uses them to fill her closet
her jewelry box
uses them to decorate her home
makes gifts of them
though she has money
a fine house
a finer man

far from immune
I have my own
blackfeathered ways
perpetually the child
who lost Christmas
I now buy willy-nilly
anything that sparkles
or shines a moment
in the light
though I worry
I won't make rent

we each apply whatever salve
we think will heal
and yet it's always there
the bloody stain
we rearrange furniture
to cover

we were each other's
unwanted mirror
reflecting memories
inflicting pain
at every chance encounter

there is no magick balm to heal
nor common thread to bind
and there cannot be kinship
among crows.

Prophecy

For Edwin Ross Martin, 1954-2010

I wonder if the dead remember
things they couldn't
when they were alive
if when breath stops
and there is perfect silence
or when the busy world
goes still and dark
the dead can suddenly see
through a glass clearly

I wonder if my brother remembers
what I could never talk about
if he recalls
how I mothered him
when I was only seven

How our sister had been struck by an army jeep
and Mother rushed to the hospital
leaving him alone

How Grandmother and I
journeyed 14 hours by bus
to a hellhole in Albany
and found him
in that trailer inferno
whimpering in his crib
face covered by insects

spoiled bottle of milk
beside him

How Grandmother left us
to search for Mother
how I'd never held a baby by myself
and I was scared

But his cries hurt me
with a new pain
so I changed his shitty diapers
like I'd seen them do
in the church nursery
I put them on lopsided
couldn't make it right
but he was dry and clean

I found a washcloth
and a bowl of warm water
to bathe his eyes
sealed shut by swarming gnats

I can still recall the feeling
of the warm cloth
taking away the filth
his infant loneliness and fear
each ragged breath
those snuffling cries
that shook us both
then his eyes opened

and I thought he smiled
at me

I poured him a fresh bottle
and didn't know to warm it
but held him like my Tiny Tears doll
and sang and rocked back and forth
Hush little baby, don't say a word
and he drank it down fast
even though it was cold

I sang till Grandmother came back
she wasn't surprised
that I'd done all that
didn't even say
what a smart girl you are

Instead, she looked at me
as though she wasn't certain
that what I'd done was very smart at all

as though what she saw
frightened her somehow

the way you get chills for no reason
when you hear the mournful whistle of a train
or a crow's call
as the sun bleeds
down the sky at dusk
and you just know
it can't mean anything good.

Endangered

My mother's children have begun to die
we who were pushed from a common womb

golden lion tamarin and arctic fox
panda, polar bear, koala

the call comes
never when you're ready

the very bones of my mother
her coral reefs
dying with clown fish and the seahorse
who swam between her great ribs

the call that comes
in the middle of the night

my brothers and sisters have begun to die
they who harmed no one

emperor penguin
and the little mariana fruit bat

the call with its hospital background noises
broken voice jagged

brothers and sisters
children of my mother are dying

anaconda and frogs and brightfeathered wonders
tangled in her rainforest hair

the call comes

my brother is dead
that cold sliver of a soul
last seen bronzed and shining
clothed in white linen
a danger
a stranger
an anger
bloody and raw

the call comes
a danger a stranger

my mother's children have begun to die
incapable of hate
they blink out innocent
not to return

mountain gorilla and macaque
blue-eyed black lemur
arctic wolf
and the strong Siberian tiger

the call comes
and whom shall I mourn?

Lamb

You are the loss that hurt me
most of all
you were the lamb
whose blood still stains
my dreams
Beloved Life
your name was irony

most innocent of all
the baby
who would never be much more

and when our mother died
you flew west
to sad oblivion
where you are lost
these endless years

I had a friend
who grew up on a farm
she told me how life works
in such a place
how hatchlings
without strength
to break the shell
died locked within

how lambs
too weak to stand
were left to perish

she called it life
I call it what it is.

One flew east

postscript

When we were free
we scattered
four siblings
who entered as lambs
left as crows
bleak feathers drifting
making shadows
wherever we go

now we are three
a brother lost
to excess and oblivion
two sisters alien to me
impossible to relate
although for years
we tried

our memories
all mismatched
prickly and painful
we prefer our illusions
pray to different gods
that nothing slithers out
to plague our dreams
recall the damning truth

As the eldest
I tried to keep them

safely silent
all good children
quiet and golden
in the hiding dark
while the latest stepfather raged
or when I journeyed to bars
terrified of drunk and many-handed men
to fetch our mother at midnight

I can tell you
that in those days
we were stolen
from cribs and playpens
sandbox and swings
not by elves or faeries
but by twisted fate
innocence amputated
as though it were useless
an appendage to which
we were not entitled

and when it was all over
last grave filled
last flower placed
to wither, to die, to disappear

we flew
clutching our shiny myths
bright baubles

in selfish talons
caching them
in hidden nests
to make memories
we could live with

flying our crippled paths
on crooked wings and broken
wobbling and unable to steer
any other course but
away.

About the Poet

Nine times nominated for The Pushcart Prize, Carla Martin-Wood is the author of the recently released *Into the Windfall Light* from The Pink Petticoat Press. She is also the author of *Flight Risk & Other Poems, Songs from the Web (encore)*, and *How we are loved*, all from Fortunate Childe Publications.

She has authored seven chapbooks: *Songs from the Web* (Bitter Wine Press); *Garden of Regret* and *Redheaded Stepchild* (both Pudding House Chapbook Series); *Feed Sack Majesty, HerStory,* and *The Last Magick and Other Poems* (all Fortunate Childe Publications); and *Absinthe & Valentines* (Flutter Press).

Carla's poems have appeared in a plethora of journals and numerous anthologies in the US, England, and Ireland since 1978.

She is Copy Director of an advertising agency, and freelances book design on occasion. Carla has three magnificent granddaughters: Sarah, Erica, and Caeli Grace, in order of appearance. She was nominated for Best of the Net 2010 and 2011, and is listed in the Poets & Writers Directory at www.pw.org

Acknowledgements

Vespers at Mama-Teen's, For Montine, Fishing, from **Feed Sack Majesty,** Fortunate Childe Publications, 2009

Sunday Mom Blues, Thurisaz, Isa, Why I never visit, from **Flight Risk**, Fortunate Childe Publications, 2010

Papa's Finale, from **Garden of Regret**, Pudding House Publications, 2009

Photo of my mother at nineteen, Werewolf, Skydiver, from **Redheaded Stepchild**, Pudding House Publications, 2009

From the shadows, from **How we are loved**, Fortunate Childe Publications, 2010

Late prayer to Isis for my grandmother's soul, from **Postcards from Eve**, Fortunate Childe Publications, 2010

Also by this author

Into the Windfall Light
The Pink Petticoat Press

Flight Risk & other poems
Fortunate Childe Publications

Songs from the Web (encore)
Fortunate Childe Publications

How we are loved
Fortunate Childe Publications

Absinthe & Valentines
Flutter Press

The Last Magick
Fortunate Childe Publications

HerStory
Fortunate Childe Publications

Feed Sack Majesty
Fortunate Childe Publications

Redheaded Stepchild
Pudding House Chapbook Series

Garden of Regret
Pudding House Chapbook Series

www.ingramcontent.com/pod-product-compliance
Lightning Source LLC
LaVergne TN
LVHW021611080426
835510LV00019B/2514